THE Dragon Tarot

Nigel Suckling

Illustrated by
Roger and Linda Garland

CICO BOOKS
LONDON NEW YORK

This edition published in 2018 by CICO Books
An imprint of Ryland Peters & Small Ltd
20–21 Jockey's Fields   341 E 116th St
London WC1R 4BW   New York, NY 10029

www.rylandpeters.com

First published in 2005

10 9 8 7 6

Text © Nigel Suckling 2005
Design and illustration © CICO Books 2005, 2018

The author's moral rights have been asserted. All rights reserved. No part of this publication may be reproduced, stored in a retrieval system, or transmitted in any form or by any means, electronic, mechanical, photocopying, or otherwise, without the prior permission of the publisher.

A CIP catalog record for this book is available from the Library of Congress and the British Library.

ISBN: 978-1-78249-585-7

Printed in China

Designers: David Fordham and Emily Breen
Senior editor: Carmel Edmonds
Art director: Sally Powell
Production controller: David Hearn
Publishing manager: Penny Craig
Publisher: Cindy Richards

MIX
Paper from responsible sources
FSC® C106563

Contents

Introduction   4
The major arcana and mythic dragons   5
The minor arcana and the dragons of the four elements   6

How to Lay the Cards   8
Three-card spreads   9
Five-card spread   10
Romany seven-card pyramid   11
Ouroboros spread   12
Classic ten-card spread   13

The Major Arcana   14

The Minor Arcana   36

Acknowledgments   64

Introduction

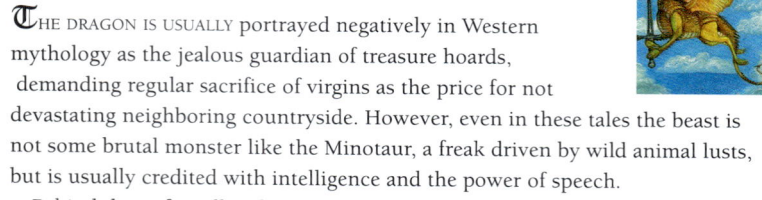

The dragon is usually portrayed negatively in Western mythology as the jealous guardian of treasure hoards, demanding regular sacrifice of virgins as the price for not devastating neighboring countryside. However, even in these tales the beast is not some brutal monster like the Minotaur, a freak driven by wild animal lusts, but is usually credited with intelligence and the power of speech.

Behind the unfriendly tales in which the dragon serves largely as a test of valor for passing knights-errant lies an esoteric tradition of the creature, embodying forces of nature that we barely understand. Although occasionally hostile, as when an Earth Dragon stirs and our cities crumble, or when Water Dragons release torrents from the sky or river, there is no personal malice. Dragons simply operate by different laws that do not automatically have at their heart human interest. Understanding and bending to their laws is one path to wisdom.

This is the spirit in which we adopted dragons as the patrons of our Tarot – because Tarot also operates by laws that lie slightly beyond our conscious grasp, lifting the veil on the hidden undercurrents of the world we inhabit.

Tarot Origins

The origins of the Tarot are mysterious. All that is certain is that Tarot decks similar to those we know today – with 56 minor arcana cards and 22 major arcana cards – have survived from fifteenth-century France and Italy.

Occultist Antoine Court de Gebelin (1725–84) advanced the theory that the cards were of Egyptian origin; in the nineteenth century Eliphas Levi (1810–75) interpreted Tarot in the light of the Jewish mystical tradition of Qabbala, relating the Major Arcana to the 22 letters of the Hebrew alphabet and the 22 paths of the Tree of Life, Qabbala's central motif.

In its long journey from ancient times to the present Tarot has absorbed all the mystical influences it has met along the way, and continues to evolve today.

The Major Arcana and Mythic Dragons

The dragon found in most classic Tarot packs is the cockatrice or basilisk, sometimes shown as an Egyptian Sphinx on the Wheel of Fortune card. With its cockerel head and feet, dragon body, tail, and wings, which could belong to either or both species, the cockatrice was anciently called King of the Serpents because it was the only creature all of them feared equally, from the lowliest grass snake to the mightiest Wyvern. In Greek mythology, basilisks were born from poultry eggs hatched by toads or serpents, and their direct gaze turned all other creatures to stone – save its nemesis, the weasel, which was immune and eager to fight it to the death. So, as King of the Serpents, the cockatrice presides over the dragons of this Tarot, ensuring that they do not overstep their limits.

On the Tower, a dragon destroys the tower on Glastonbury Tor, completing the work of its medieval forebear. A church dedicated to St Michael, the Biblical dragon-slayer, was built on top of the Tor, but the dragon fought back and on September 11, 1275 the earth shook and the church collapsed. It was rebuilt but the walls would not stay up, and all that remains now is the tower, built in 1360.

THE TOWER

The two bickering dragons on the Chariot card represent polar opposites: yin and yang, male and female, light and dark. On the World card is the Worm Ouroboros, the Norse Midgard Serpent, encircling the globe and forever feeding off its own tail. It represents, among other things, the eternal self-renewal of nature.

THE CHARIOT

The Minor Arcana and the Dragons of the Four Elements

Dragons are perfectly suited as guides to the Tarot's minor arcana due to their intrinsic link with the elements of the four suits: water, air, fire, and earth.

In the West, dragons' ancient alignment with the four elements emerged during the fifteenth and sixteenth centuries when alchemists and other fringe philosophers recorded positive associations with these mythic creatures, often in the face of Christian hostility. Alchemists regarded the dragon as non-transmuted base metal, the raw power of nature that might transform into gold, or ultimate knowledge. In alchemists' colorful treatises we meet dragons in their guises as nature's primal forces – the Dragons of the Four Elements.

Suit	Element	Dragon	Qualities	Realm
Cups	Water	Water Dragon	Love, family, protection	Emotions
Swords	Air	Air Dragon	Authority, judgment, courage	Intellect
Wands	Fire	Fire Dragon	Enterprise, creativity, practicality	Action
Pentacles	Earth	Earth Dragon	Finance, trade, business ventures	Matter

INTRODUCTION 7

THE SUIT OF CUPS

Water Dragons: Suit of Cups

Water dragons appear in ancient legend as Leviathan, ruler of the oceans, Typhon in ancient Egypt, and Tiamat in Babylon. In lesser guises they emerge as lindworm, who in Europe dwell in every lake, river, and stream, including the famous Lambton Worm of England.

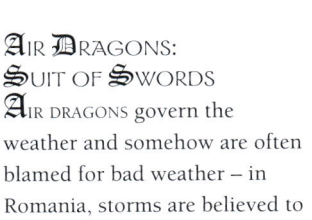

Air Dragons: Suit of Swords

Air dragons govern the weather and somehow are often blamed for bad weather – in Romania, storms are believed to be caused by evil wizards flying dragons, and hurricanes are so-called after the dragon-like Central American weather-god, Huracan.

THE SUIT OF SWORDS

Fire Dragons: Suit of Wands

Fire dragons, or drakes, range from the humble salamander to the multi-headed dragon Typhoeus that Zeus imprisoned under Mount Etna. To this day the dragon struggles to break free, causing eruptions and devastation.

THE SUIT OF WANDS

Earth Dragons: Suit of Pentacles

Earth dragons guard their treasure in caves, yet they represent not malice or greed but simply the dormant abundance of the earth. The most famous dragon of ancient Greece was Ladon, who guarded the Golden Apples of the Hesperides and was slain by Hercules.

THE SUIT OF PENTACLES

THE DRAGON TAROT

How to Lay the Cards

There are countless ways of spreading the cards for a reading, and it is worth experimenting to find those that suit you best. Here are five popular, effective spreads that cover most people's needs. It is quite all right to use just the 22 Major Arcana cards to begin with, especially for the simple three- and five-card spreads; novices often find this a fast way to become familiar with the major cards. Also, bear in mind that reversed cards can usually be regarded as a guide and measure of effort needed to attain their upright value. If you are reading for someone else, it is usual to sit opposite them and let them shuffle and cut the cards while imprinting their energy on the cards, before you lay them out.

Getting Started

When reading for yourself, shuffle the cards well, concentrating on the situation or dilemma foremost in your mind. Phrase your question clearly, or better still write down the question and its response; be as specific as you can. Cut the deck into three piles and pick them up in the order shown, with the center pile on top. For every spread, lay the cards face down and turn each one over horizontally, like the pages of a book, then refer to the meanings on pages 14–63.

Lay three piles from left to right as shown, then replace the deck in the order 2, 3, 1, so the center pile 2 is on top, pile 3 is under it, and pile 1 is on the bottom.

Three-Card Spreads

There are times when life is too busy for a detailed reading, but it is helpful to have a quick glimpse into the nature and prospects of the situation we find ourselves in. Here's a very simple spread that offers just that.

Shuffle the cards as described on page 8, concentrating on your question as you do so. Lay out the top three, face down, then turn them over.

1 Past    2 Present    3 Future

The first card represents the past, the circumstances that have created the situation you are in. The second card represents that situation at present, and the third card stands for the future, the likely outcome.

Alternatively, you can read the three cards another way. The first card now represents the situation, the second card represents the challenge or obstacle to be overcome, and the third card stands for the likely outcome.

1 Situation    2 Challenge    3 Outcome

Five-Card Spread

The Five-card Spread gives more detail than the three-card spreads (see page 9), while still being quick enough for questioners in a hurry. It is particularly well suited for simple, well-defined situations with clear options.

Shuffle and cut the cards as described on page 8 and lay down the top five, face down, in the order shown below:

Card 1:
The card in the center represents the overall nature of the situation.

Card 4:
The recent past – the underlying, practical causes of the situation.

Card 3:
Past influences behind the situation – the psychological climate that has brought it about.

Card 5:
Future influences – how you will feel about the outcome and how it will affect your relations with the world.

Card 2:
The likely practical outcome.

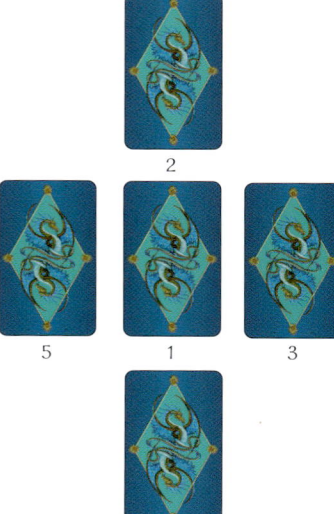

Romany Seven-Card Pyramid

THIS SPREAD IS IDEAL for questioners who feel that others may misunderstand their aims. One line of cards deals with internal, subjective factors while the other concerns external, objective ones. Between them, they can give a broad and clear overview of the way ahead. Shuffle and cut the cards as described on page 8 and lay down the first seven, face down, in the order shown below:

CARD 1:
The key card representing your current predicament and mood.

CARD 2:
How you appear to those you are trying to influence.

CARD 3:
Your true feelings, the person behind the persona.

CARD 4:
Action to resolve the situation.

CARD 5:
How you will feel about the necessary action.

CARD 6:
The likely outcome.

CARD 7:
How you will feel about the outcome.

OUROBOROS SPREAD

NAMED AFTER THE TAIL-EATING World Serpent, which the circular spread of seven cards resembles, this spread is useful when you are looking for a simple "yes" or "no" answer, as it presents the progression of events as a time-line.

Shuffle and cut the deck, laying out the cards as shown below.

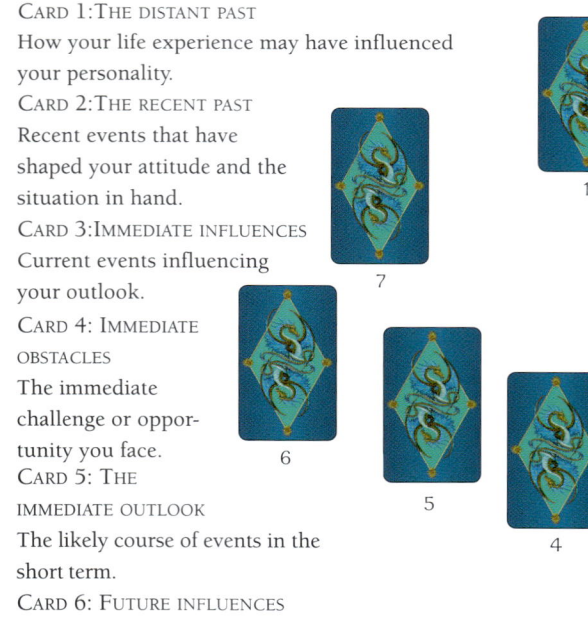

CARD 1: THE DISTANT PAST
How your life experience may have influenced your personality.

CARD 2: THE RECENT PAST
Recent events that have shaped your attitude and the situation in hand.

CARD 3: IMMEDIATE INFLUENCES
Current events influencing your outlook.

CARD 4: IMMEDIATE OBSTACLES
The immediate challenge or opportunity you face.

CARD 5: THE IMMEDIATE OUTLOOK
The likely course of events in the short term.

CARD 6: FUTURE INFLUENCES
How current choices affect your relationship with the world.

CARD 7: THE ULTIMATE OUTCOME
The culmination of all the previous cards and the likely long-term result.

Alternatively, you can use this spread to predict the fortunes of the week ahead with card 1 representing Monday, through card 7 for Sunday.

Classic Ten-Card Spread

The first six cards give an overall picture of the current situation and its likely outcome, and the next four (cards 7–10) reprise it from a different perspective for fresh insight.

Shuffle and cut the deck, laying out the cards as shown below.

Card 1: The current situation
You and your current situation.
Card 2: Obstacles or supports
The greatest immediate challenge you face in achieving your desires.
Card 3: Destiny
The likely outcome – if you are to achieve your goal.
Card 4: Foundations
The psychological background to the situation.
Card 5: The recent past
The recent, practical causes of the situation.
Card 6: Influence
How the outcome may influence how you feel about your life as a whole.

Card 7: The questioner
How you see yourself in relation to the problem.
Card 8: The environment
How others see you.

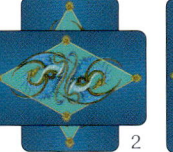

Card 9: Inner emotions
Your inner hopes and fears, and other emotions at play here.
Card 10: Result
The likely outcome.

0 THE FOOL

CARELESSNESS
FRIVOLITY
IMMATURITY
SPONTANEITY

THE FOOL represents the wild optimism of youth, rushing into adventures with no thought for the consequences. Although this impulsiveness often leads to disaster, especially in mature people who should know better, it is what makes the world turn. The dragonet snapping at the Fool's foot symbolizes his cautious conscience, warning him not to get too carried away and fall off the edge.

UPRIGHT MEANING

A new beginning with fresh adventures ahead, although there is a very real danger of it all going horribly wrong. The bag on the Fool's shoulder represents natural talents that he could employ usefully if he took the trouble to open the bag, but he generally doesn't. For wild optimists this card is a warning to try to temper enthusiasms with a little common sense. For pessimists, it suggests lightening up a little.

REVERSED MEANING

This is an unlucky warning of imminent disaster unless the person it refers to pulls themselves together and starts acting responsibly. All the Fool's worst qualities of fecklessness and lack of commitment are about to demand a heavy price. His confidence will prove hollow.

1 The Magician

CREATIVITY
ELOQUENCE
CONFIDENCE
ORIGINALITY
MAGIC

With one hand on the wand, the Magician gazes thoughtfully down at the symbols of the four Tarot suits, contemplating his next move. They are emblems of the four elements, whose interactions create the endless variety of life; and by the judicious balancing of one against the other, enchantment can be brought into the world. The Magician is related to Hermes the messenger, patron of tricksters and alchemists.

Upright Meaning

This card signals originality and inventiveness. This is a lucky time for new undertakings. Everything will come together, and when you speak you will be believed because of your evident sense. Inspiration, too, will come when you most need it, helping you tackle unforeseen challenges. This is a good time to travel and favors any travel plans you have.

Reversed Meaning

Lack of confidence, vision, and persuasiveness combine to produce confusion and failure; or someone close is playing tricks and is not who they seem. Either way, this is a bad omen for new ventures and caution is urged. It pays to discuss plans with trusted friends.

II THE HIGH PRIESTESS

WISDOM
INTUITION
MYSTICISM
SECRECY

THE HIGH PRIESTESS is often equated with the Moon, or the veiled Isis, sister and wife of Osiris in ancient Egyptian myth. The book from which she is reading contains all the mysteries of both life and death, which she guards and shares with her initiates. Although a good teacher, she is also a slightly remote, self-contained figure who usually requires the help of more practical spirits to make her insights function in reality.

UPRIGHT MEANING

Inspiration, learning, mystery, understanding of the inner workings of life, enlightenment, and serenity are all represented by this card, with a hint that serenity can sometimes lead to emotional detachment from daily events. Often this card implies that hidden spiritual factors are currently affecting your life, so look carefully within, or consult a respected advisor.

REVERSED MEANING

Reversed, the card stands for shallowness, delusion, and selfishness – the tendency to assume that one is always right, despite contrary evidence. Poor judgment follows from a gullible acceptance of wishful occult thinking.

III The Empress

FERTILITY
SUCCESS
HARMONY
SENSUALITY

As the High Priestess stands at the gate of the Otherworld, the Empress guards over this one. She represents the middle aspect of the triple goddess who as Venus seduces man with her delicate charms, as Gaia or Demeter tends the garden of this world in which children grow to maturity, and as Isis ushers them into the next. The Empress is the ideal, selfless mother.

Upright Meaning

A mother or mother-figure, either a symbol of one's own mother or a reminder of the ideal. However, this card can simply signal a time of fertility and abundance. As a ruler the Empress is wise, generous, and scrupulously fair, giving a lead by subtle hint and example rather than direct order. This card suggests action and worldly success for any imminent enterprise, whether it be marriage, work, or art.

Reversed Meaning

In her negative aspect the Empress can be vacillating, domineering, over-possessive, devious, vindictive, and jealous. This is the card of partnerships that have turned sour, either in family or work, and little good will come of it until the relationship is either brought back into balance, or ended.

IV The Emperor

POWER
CONFIDENCE
STRENGTH
HONESTY

Where the Emperor differs most from the Empress, his consort, is in the directness of his approach to problems. He rules by decree and command, quick and confident in his wisdom and sense of justice. He is ambitious and will stop at nothing to achieve his aims. This card represents will and confident authority.

Upright Meaning

The Emperor represents earthly power achieved through force of will, including war if necessary, though usually the card stands for stability, wealth, justice and the dominance of reason over emotion. It can represent an authority figure at work or in the family, or the attitude necessary to carry plans through to fruition. Sometimes it's necessary to put aside reflection and sympathy, and simply act.

Reversed Meaning

Reversed, the Emperor card can represent either difficulty with an outside authority or possibly indicate one's own abuse of power. The reversed Emperor is a confused, immature bully. Look hard in the mirror before deciding to whom the card refers, because it is much easier to project these qualities onto others than to own up to them.

V The Hierophant

TRADITION
COMMUNITY
CHARITY
CONSERVATISM

The Hierophant represents a leader of established religion. He is the natural counterpart of The High Priestess, but he has formal and even political power that often blinds him to the spiritual values he guards. While often providing real community comfort to his followers, obsession with history and tradition often blinds him to new spiritual developments.

Upright Meaning

Providing comfort, security, the wisdom of the ages, and generosity in others' time of need are among the many virtues of the Hierophant that make him someone to turn to in troubled times. But inflexibility – a lack of openness to change – can often negate these virtues. Too great a reverence for the past can become hostility toward all change, and then the Hierophant symbolizes an obstacle to growth. He can also indicate marriage or other lasting union.

Reversed Meaning

Reversed, the Hierophant becomes unconventional but also weak, gullible, and unreliable. In a spread, this card often indicates a need for unconventional solutions, but may warn of treachery from colleagues and superiors. Postpone long-term commitments until the situation clears.

VI The Lovers

Decision
Devotion
Love
Infatuation

The young couple joining hands within the dragon's embrace are entering the adventure of a shared life, buoyed by the optimism of youth and within the embrace of high wisdom. There may be troubles ahead, but for now the pair take simple joy in each other's company, confident that together they will be a match for anything that comes. The card suggests a happy union in either the private or work spheres.

Upright Meaning
Generally this card represents love or friendship on the worldly plane, marking a kindling or re-kindling of affection after troubles have been overcome. A major commitment could seriously affect the course of your life, and the climate is right for it to be a lasting and fruitful union. Complete honesty and trust are all that are needed to make the union work.

Reversed Meaning
Reversed, the card warns of heartache, disappointment, failure, and possible betrayal by a friend or lover. To cope you need to be cautious, consistent, and persevering, and plan wisely. Say what you mean and mean what you say, as this is no time for lazy assumptions or half-hearted commitments.

VII The Chariot

ADVENTURE
DANGER
EXCITEMENT
TRIUMPH
DETERMINATION

THE CHARIOT SHOWS a young man hurtling along on a great adventure, drawn by two powerful yet quarrelsome dragons that require all his strength and determination to control. Like yin and yang, they represent qualities that are neither good nor bad in themselves, but which naturally tend to clash and get out of balance.

Upright Meaning
Triumph through the careful balancing of opposites and courage in the face of danger are shown by this card. Turmoil, upheaval, and excitement on a journey that can be metaphorical or real, but either way leave you feeling that you have arrived in a different place. Hard work at this stage is recognized and rewarded for a change, but be careful not to relax too soon.

Reversed Meaning
Discouragement, quarrels, and defeat are indicated by the card in the reversed position. The charioteer fails to control his fractious steeds and plunges to disaster. Great undertakings need loyal allies and a firm grasp of detail which, if overlooked, can bring the dream crashing down. This card can indicate a journey beset by delays, or becomes a flight from reality.

VIII JUSTICE

FAIRNESS
EQUALITY
HARMONY
BALANCE
IMPARTIALITY

LIFE IS OFTEN UNFAIR, and luck counts for more than we care to admit in realizing our dreams. Opposed to this, however, is the natural human thirst for fairness represented by the eighth card of the Major Arcana which recalls Themis, the ancient Greek goddess of Justice, with her scales and her sword of discernment, in this case supported by the dragon of higher wisdom. She represents an ideal that we may strive toward.

UPRIGHT MEANING

Justice reveals a judgment in your favor as you receive your just rewards. This can be uncomfortable for those who have strayed beyond morality, but usually this card signals good fortune for you and a happy outcome to current negotiations. The card signals a good time for drawing up contracts, settling outstanding debts and obligations, and laying foundations for the future.

REVERSED MEANING

Loss, particularly in legal matters, injustice, and lack of recognition at work are all threatened by the Justice card reversed. Prepare to ride out a storm as false accusations, prejudice, and bullying may come your way, but try to see this as a test of character.

IX THE HERMIT

WISDOM
SOLITUDE
DETACHMENT
MYSTICISM

THE HERMIT GUARDS ancient esoteric truths nurtured and harvested away from the bustle of everyday life. He seeks his own path through dark, little frequented byways of the human soul. His patient introspection uncovers secrets of the soul that the turmoil of daily life tends to obscure, and whose importance often only manifests in times of trouble.

UPRIGHT MEANING

The Hermit in a reading can represent either the attitude required of the questioner in the current situation, or someone nearby with the detachment to see the way forward. Prudence, patience, and caution are all suggested by this card, and also a need for withdrawal and contemplation. Don't rush into anything until you properly understand what is going on. Be more eager to listen than to speak.

REVERSED MEANING

Reversed, the Hermit represents over-caution, enforced solitude, timidity, and fear of facing the world and honestly interacting with others. His meditations are an indulgence and excuse for avoiding life, and he misses chances to help others with his knowledge through hesitation, clumsiness, and lack of empathy.

X The Wheel of Fortune

LUCK
COINCIDENCE
CHANGE
DESTINY

The Wheel of Fortune represents the ever-turning balance of impersonal forces that shape our lives independently of all conscious aims and effort. There are times in life when everything goes right (or wrong) purely through seemingly chance events beyond our control. At such moments we are at the mercy of fortune, ruled by the cockatrice or basilisk at the top whose sword ensures no one basks in glory or defeat too long.

Upright Meaning
Good luck, change, and a revolution in your fortunes. Forgotten friends and unexpected allies suddenly appear to help realize some of your dreams. Strange coincidences also work in your favor. Make the most of it, but beware of pride and conceit. Remember to share your windfall with all who help make it happen, and bear in mind that it will not last forever.

Reversed Meaning
Bad luck, obstruction, betrayal, and indifference all conspire to bring you to a standstill. This is a bad time for new undertakings and also for gambling. Concentrate on small, practical achievements that will bear fruit. Practice cheerfulness in the face of adversity. It will pass.

XI Strength

Power
Determination
Tenacity
Courage

The female subduing the dragon represents humanity taming its wilder instincts and channeling them to useful purpose. Unlike St George who merely killed his dragon, she tames hers and gains its respect, adding its strengths to her own and becoming invincible. She is related to Artemis, or Diana the Huntress, and other pagan Queens of the Beasts.

Upright Meaning

This card signifies success through meeting problems head-on and overcoming them by strength of will. Perseverance, courage, and determination combined with intelligence and modesty make an irresistible combination not only for tackling adversity but for encouraging others to come to your assistance. The strength of this card inspires others because its triumph benefits all.

Reversed Meaning

Strength reversed reveals wasted effort, failure, and the possible alienation of others through the abuse of power. In the reversed card the dragon has won the battle and the woman has become tainted by self-interest. By losing sight of any larger goal she loses the sympathy and the support of others. Here, restraint, modesty, and patience are called for.

XII THE HANGED MAN

SELF-SACRIFICE
ORIGINALITY
BALANCE
REBIRTH

As with the Death card, the Hanged Man is much less ominous than he first appears. Although suspended over an abyss, our man is serene and seems almost to be enjoying his novel view of the world, perhaps because he knows it will give fresh insights when he is back on his feet again. Like the Fool, he cares little for dignity or even danger, and trusts in a higher wisdom to show him the way.

UPRIGHT MEANING
You are at a life crossroads at which sacrifices and patience are needed if the right choices are to be made. Submit gracefully, and all will be well. Life needs to be viewed from a fresh angle, and what may seem a total distraction to your plans may just take you in a fresh, creative direction. You may feel you are wasting time hanging around, but it will prove to be well worth your while.

REVERSED MEANING
Beware of pointless time-wasting, selfishness, and half-hearted sacrifice that achieves nothing. You need to find new ways of dealing with events. The card may also warn of accidents, danger, and loss. Remember that whatever fails to break you only makes you stronger.

XIII DEATH

CHANGE
LOSS
UPHEAVAL
RENEWAL

FEW PEOPLE RELISH the appearance of Death, but it is rarely a warning of physical death. This unlucky thirteenth card can represent calamity and endings, but mostly it signals fresh beginnings, for which something has to give way. The card signals the passage from one stage of life to another, which may involve sacrifice and pain, but there is no other way to renewal.

UPRIGHT MEANING

This card represents a creative revolution or transformation of life, probably involving the loss of friendly, family, or business connections, but only as the prelude to a fresh and rewarding phase of life. In physical health it can warn of a potential crisis if you pay no attention to warning signals, but the card is more usually concerned with spiritual health and the need for periodic renewal to avoid stagnation.

REVERSED MEANING

The reversed Death card is bad news, but rarely is its message catastrophic. It warns of lethargy, inertia, and resistance to change, leading to exhaustion and standstill. Clinging too much to the past can lead to an inability to adapt to changing conditions. Beware of becoming a caricature of your old self.

XIV TEMPERANCE

WISDOM
PATIENCE
TOLERANCE
CONFIDENCE

THE ANGEL OF TIME carefully pours the Water of Life from one vase into the other, signifying on one level the blending of past and present to produce understanding with depth. The pouring can also signify the blending of spirit and matter, and the reverse, leading to fruitfulness and prosperity. The dragon in the background is keeping guard so that life can prosper in the sheltered valley.

UPRIGHT MEANING

Discipline, patience, restraint, and thoughtfulness lead to happiness and quiet success. Creativity and contentment go hand in hand. This is not a card of fame and glory, but of the simple pleasures of daily life properly appreciated. It represents compromise in its most creative sense, and the ideal conditions for raising a family or cultivating a long-term career.

REVERSED MEANING

Disunion, overwork, competing interests, dissipation, restlessness, and waste can all lead to a feeling of exhaustion. Nothing seems to have any real meaning, and if the mood persists long enough, friends will begin to fall away. The past feels like a burden because you are unable to learn from it.

XV The Devil

TEMPTATION
OBSESSION
LUST
DELUSION
ENTRAPMENT

Like the Death and Hanged Man cards, to the uninitiated the Devil is far less ominous than he first appears. However, his arrival in a reading does warn of the very real danger of being led astray by false lights, empty promises, or shallow pleasures. Enslavement of one sort or another is threatened by the Devil, who often comes in the most seductive of guises, but you can choose how you respond to his advances.

Upright Meaning

Whether or not you are fully conscious of it, you or someone in close proximity are already bound to some self-destructive attachment that can only end in tears. It is time to listen to your own inner voice of wisdom and a way out will soon become clear. The misfortune threatened by this card is not a force of nature, but a consequence of choice.

Reversed Meaning

The reversed card signifies the end of an ill-starred period of delusion, when it's time to crawl from the ruins and begin again. There is still some danger, but if you listen to the promptings of the angel on one shoulder and ignore the devil on the other, you can find renewal.

XVI The Tower

Shock
Revolution
Loss
Uncertainty

The Tower of stale, outmoded belief is toppled by the Dragon of repressed natural instincts. The falling figures represent the plunge into confusion that comes with the shattering of long-held convictions. They also reflect Adam and Eve, cast out of Eden into the mortal world, having for the first time to feed and clothe themselves, or children being cast out of the home.

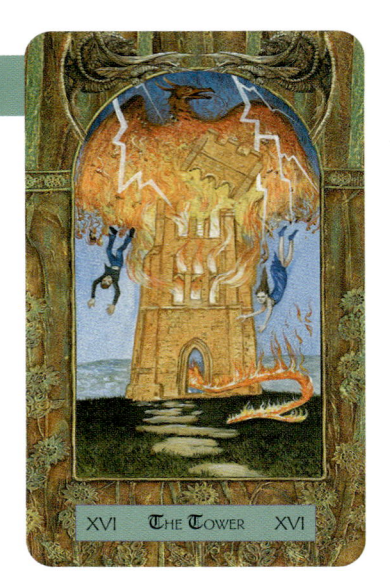

Upright Meaning

Without warning the old order breaks down and chaos breaks loose. Upheaval, betrayal, and failure all threaten to shake your self-belief. This is a common card for people facing the challenges of mid-life, although love can create similar havoc at any age, as can politics, war, and business. Such revolutions always lead to clearer understanding in the long term, however.

Reversed Meaning

Reversed, the shock is considerably lessened, but still demands great and flexible character and patience to withstand. Be open to change and a re-evaluation of your ideals, but keep those roots firmly clinging to the remaining certainties of your life. Friends prove their worth in times like this, but beware of imposing too much on their patience.

XVII The Star

Hope
Rebirth
Inspiration
Truth

Like that of the Magi over Bethlehem, the great Star is the portent of a new beginning. The change will take time to manifest, but this most optimistic card signals the return of hope after a period of trial and tribulation. The dragon pouring Water of Life into the lake and onto the land is Truth, whose blinding clarity lights the path from trouble to peace.

Upright Meaning

Like the return of spring after winter, the Star signals rebirth in any or all aspects of life, and the relaxing of restraints. After an illness, The Star card indicates the return of health. After a period of frustration in relationships or work, it promises the return of joy and the blossoming of new partnerships. This is a good time to begin any new venture, and also to travel.

Reversed Meaning

When reversed, the card signals failure, wrong choices, disappointment, and confusion. Although it stops short of promising imminent disaster, the Star reversed warns of the danger of trusting to false promises and unrealistic schemes that will lead nowhere. Optimism is usually a blessing, but when it is ungrounded in reality it can become a curse.

XVIII THE MOON

IMAGINATION
MYSTERY
DILEMMA
DANGER
ILLUSION

THE MOON OF INSPIRATION rises over the gateway to the unconscious while dragons serenade it and the crab or crayfish of Cancer hesitates, scared of leaving its natural medium. This card suggests the need to shake off convention and follow your instincts and intuitions. Pay attention to your dreams, because they will be full of hints of how to address the major issue that has arisen, or is about to.

UPRIGHT MEANING

A choice needs to be made that could determine your happiness for a long time ahead. You need to be guided by intuition and feelings when making this choice, but at the same time there is a real danger of delusion, of being misled by wishful thinking, or by someone whose judgment you trust. Times like this are true tests of character and your grasp on reality.

REVERSED MEANING

Confusion, uncertainty, misjudgment, and deception all bring a feeling of chaos, even madness, into your life, but there is no great danger of it getting serious. Health could also be a worry, but on all fronts patience and rest are the best remedies. Content yourself with small achievements until the mood passes.

THE MAJOR ARCANA 33

XIX THE SUN

LUCK
PEACE
PLENTY
CONTENTMENT
GROWTH

THE SUN RADIATES ITS BLESSING upon the world, its benevolent dragon breathing warmth and life into nature. The garden wall by which the children happily play signifies the shelter provided by an ordered world. The card symbolizes the joys of peace and civilization that allow all things, not least the arts, to bloom. Amid such conditions almost any new enterprise you contemplate will flourish.

UPRIGHT MEANING

Good fortune, material success, energy, and joy are all promised by this card as whatever you undertake is blessed. New beginnings are suggested by the children and the sunflowers craning for the sky. This is a good time for new partnerships in all spheres of life and for refreshing your spirits through simple enjoyment of the good things on offer.

REVERSED MEANING

There is a great and achievable ambition almost within your grasp, but obstacles block the way. Perseverance is called for, and careful planning. This is no time for great leaps forward, but for concentrating on one sure step at a time and being patient about your goal.

xx Judgment

CONCLUSION
CHANGE
EVALUATION
DECISIVENESS

The Angel Gabriel calls the world to Judgment and the birth of a new age. A line is drawn under the past and accounts are settled as the foundation for a fresh start in life. This could signal a promotion at work or branching out in a new direction. Either way, a fresh approach to life is needed, so now is the time to measure your strengths and address your weaknesses in preparation for the future.

Upright Meaning
This card signals the ending of one stage of life and beginning of another. It is a moment for reflection and self-judgment, measuring what you have achieved against the ideals that you were aiming for, because fresh opportunities to achieve them will arise. Armed with honest self-appraisal, you will be best poised to take advantage of them. Meanwhile, it pays to be generous in your judgment of others.

Reversed Meaning
A change for the worse: delay, loss, separation, and stagnation are all suggested by the reversed card. Fear of change only worsens the situation, because hesitation leads to loss of control over events. If you avoid making decisions, others will do it for you, to your loss.

XXI The World

COMPLETION
RESOLUTION
SUCCESS
GOOD LUCK

As the last card of the Major Arcana, the World signifies completion, the achievement of ambitions, and success in the eyes of others. The Wyrm Ouroboros encircles the world to show the endless self-renewal of nature, flanked in the four corners by the dragons of the four Minor Arcana suits: Air (Swords), Water (Cups), Fire (Wands), and Earth (Pentacles).

Upright Meaning

Upright, the World represents the favorable culmination of a long period of striving and hard work that meets at last with recognition and reward. It stands for completion, fulfillment, and the dawn of a period during which you can relax and refresh yourself before the need for major exertion rises again. This is a good time to take stock and catch up on neglected areas of your life.

Reversed Meaning

The World in the reversed position warns of disappointment, a lack of imagination, and failure to carry projects right through to the end. Much more perseverance, determination, and imagination are now needed if you hope to realize any of your dreams. Stagnation is bound to set in if you don't keep supplying fresh energy to your undertakings.

Ace of Swords

Upright: The Ace of Swords signifies triumph through strength and determination, particularly in the intellectual or inventive spheres. It marks the beginning of a fresh era, a promotion perhaps, or some other kind of advancement. A danger of the intellectualism symbolized by Swords is that it can be applied equally to right and wrong causes, so you need to examine your true motives with care.

Reversed: The Ace of Swords represents danger, and the possible collapse of your dreams through arrogance and insensitivity. But it must be remembered that often grim endings are needed before fresh beginnings. Plan for the long term.

Two of Swords

Upright: Friendship, including possible reconciliation with an old enemy, shows the way forward. Often the most fruitful partnerships are those based upon underlying conflict because that way all the angles are covered, whereas like-minded people can simply reinforce each other's prejudices and only later discover their limitations in the wider world.

Reversed: An old enemy or rival offers a truce, but they are not being completely honest. Falsehood and duplicity are suggested by this card, and someone will let you down. Tread carefully; have several escape routes planned.

Three of Swords

UPRIGHT: Argument and strife threaten your plans. Be patient. Separation, frustration, and disillusionment all threaten, but if you hold onto your long-term goals they can still be realized – you just have to work out who your real friends are. Break-ups are always painful, but totally necessary in the long run.

REVERSED: Disillusionment and the ending of partnerships, either in business or in love relationships. Confusion and even madness threaten to take hold, so take care not to aggravate the situation by foolish behavior. Above all, try to be honest with yourself.

Four of Swords

UPRIGHT: A temporary relief from struggle. Use solitude to plan a way forward because the chances are that much will be demanded of you again soon. This can refer to either health or your personal life. Remember, with hindsight all the best achievements involve triumph over adversity.

REVERSED: Economy and good management are needed just now and will lead to certain success in the future, beyond the difficulties you immediately face. Defeat and loneliness loom if you do not make the effort to reach out to friends. This requires humility, but it is no bad thing. At times like this you will find out who your true friends are, and the others hardly matter.

Five of Swords

UPRIGHT: Destruction, waste, and loss threaten to undermine your spirits, but do bear in mind that they are only temporary. You may justly be feeling bad, but beware of getting caught up in a negative spiral. The conditions will pass, and you can still achieve your goals if you learn the lessons of the current setback and apply them next time around.

REVERSED: Betrayal either tempts or threatens, but should be ignored. Admitting to your own shortcomings is always a good way to undermine criticism, and gloating over others' discomfort always backfires, so just be patient.

Six of Swords

UPRIGHT: The Six reveals unexpected developments, possibly a journey or business opportunity that will open the way to realizing your ambitions in a surprising way. Leap at the chance whatever the immediate obstacles; this is not the time for hesitation or counting the pennies. In the long term it will feel worthwhile.

REVERSED: Some kind of declaration will signal the beginning of a whole new way of life. Your situation may feel like a stalemate, but know that it is about to change – just be ready to seize the moment. Remember that your determined effort always bears fruit.

Seven of Swords

Upright: Hope appears after a long struggle, but keep your guard up. You face opposition to your plans and it would be wise to learn its source, but you can achieve your aims if you persevere and be certain of your facts. Avoid direct confrontation, however; instead, let your ideas speak for themselves.

Reversed: You face a setback to your plans and even face possible betrayal by a partner or a business colleague – however, don't allow yourself to become disheartened by this negative behavior. Seek advice from those who have been through what you are facing now.

Eight of Swords

Upright: Criticism, blame, or possible illness frustrate your plans and require patience to overcome. Judgment is tried and tested at times like this, but it is important to remember that there is no better way to test the value of your beliefs, especially if you have the humility to adapt them to reality.

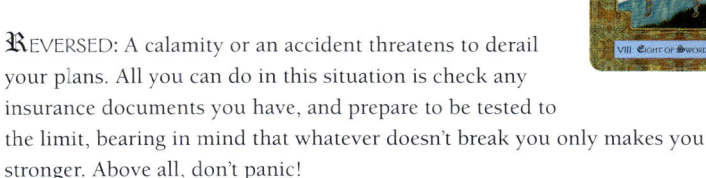

Reversed: A calamity or an accident threatens to derail your plans. All you can do in this situation is check any insurance documents you have, and prepare to be tested to the limit, bearing in mind that whatever doesn't break you only makes you stronger. Above all, don't panic!

Nine of Swords

UPRIGHT: Beware tempting but false invitations. Deception and even possible violence are warned by this card, but bear in mind that adversity is the best test of character, just as a sword requires fire and hammering to get a sharp edge. In the long run, know that all adversity can be turned to the good.

REVERSED: There is a real danger of getting drawn into a feud now and, as a consequence, having your confidence undermined by betrayal and malicious gossip. This is a time for turning to your true friends, and accepting that sometimes everyone needs a helping hand.

Ten of Swords

UPRIGHT: Traditionally this is the unluckiest card in the Tarot pack, being the ruling number of the unluckiest suit. As such it signals calamity on almost any front – health, finances, or romance – but it can also mean the ending of pointless commitments and the beginning of a fresh and wonderful stage of your life.

REVERSED: A slight but temporary illusion of success is forecast when the card is in this position. However, misfortune will follow if you do not take advantage of this reprieve and build up your defenses against disasters that almost certainly lie in wait just around the corner.

Page of Swords

UPRIGHT: The Page of Swords represents someone who is adept at uncovering secrets and unravelling mysteries – a problem-solver, sleuth, and possibly even a spy. He can be trusted with secrets when given good reason. He is a good diplomat with a keen eye for creative compromise, able to act on his own initiative, and only give away what is necessary to achieve a goal. His taste for secrecy can be taken too far, however.

REVERSED: The card represents a nasty surprise because of someone's deviousness, dishonesty, and false friendship. Their discretion has become a love of secrecy in itself and for the power it gives over others.

Knight of Swords

UPRIGHT: The Knight of Swords is bold and enthusiastic, but also imaginative and clever like his Queen. He is a great champion of good causes and inspires others by his idealism and dedication to any cause he adopts. He is decisive and, while others dither over a course of action, he will just plunge headlong into it and generally win the day. He is a symbol of creative upheaval, usually leading to success.

REVERSED: This card represents arrogance, recklessness, and misguided aggression. Instead of the courage to do battle if necessary, the Knight has become addicted to the thrill of fighting for its own sake.

Queen of Swords

Upright: Mystical, proud, mysterious, and sad, the Queen of Swords is the guardian of the secret wisdom of age. She signals that it is time to trust your intuition and act decisively. Put aside all minor quarrels, because this is no time for pettiness. She is also queen of winter, night, and the moon. She is often linked with mourning, but bears herself with serenity, having transmuted sorrow into wisdom.

Reversed: The card represents bad luck through a treacherous, spiteful, malicious, and bigoted person. They are skilled at manipulation and the subtleties of sarcasm. Beware of letting such a person get too close.

King of Swords

Upright: In astrology the character of Saturn in his benign aspect closely resembles that of the King of Swords. He represents power, authority, and the law, splitting complex arguments with the edge of his sword. His judgments can at times seem lacking in tolerance of human frailty, but are never unfair. The card usually represents an authority figure that the querent can look to for justice.

Reversed: The card signifies oppression, miserliness, loss, gloom, and even cruelty. This King represents a dangerous enemy that you may have to confront and either conquer or outwit to get a fair deal.

Ace of Cups

Upright: The Ace of Cups represents the beginning of a period of joy, abundance, friendship, fertility, love, and just about every other good thing you can think of on the emotional plane. It stands for the promise of being able to act out your dreams in a period of happy creativity while enjoying yourself along the way and being appreciated by those around you. Nonetheless, it will call upon all your finest qualities.

Reversed: The Ace represents the exact opposite of the upright meaning – emotional upheaval, sterility, relationship break-up, the collapse of hopes, betrayal, and insecurity, especially in personal relationships. Summon your inner strengths.

Two of Cups

Upright: Friendship and romance are in the air. New and profitable partnerships at work are also likely and could change the long-term direction of your life. The beginning of any relationship lays its foundations and shapes its development, so now is a time for putting aside all selfish and petty urges. Be your best self, and it will bring out the best in others.

Reversed: Disappointment, quarrels, and misunderstandings threaten to end in the breakdown of partnerships in either love or work. Beware of rash decisions you will later regret. It's worth trying to work through the difficulties first.

Three of Cups

Upright: A fresh start leading to success is offered. Problems that have been troubling you for a while will finally be resolved, leading to a renewed sense of purpose and direction. This card can signal the birth of a child, new love, friendship, or even career; whichever it is will lead to joy and a feeling of abundance.

Reversed: Disgrace and misfortune threaten as a result of over-indulgence and laziness. Selfishness threatens to sour a marriage or other close relationship. Although it is always hard to accept blame in these matters, it is time to take a long, hard look in the mirror.

Four of Cups

Upright: Stagnation and discontent in love matters could open the way for a rival and lead to separation and loss. Try to inject fresh life into your romance or risk losing it and only appreciating its value too late. No one likes being taken for granted or made to feel boring, and that applies to your partner as much as yourself.

Reversed: New and rewarding friendships will help blow the cobwebs out of your life and suggest novel solutions to several long-standing problems. However, do beware over-indulgence that could threaten your health.

Five of Cups

UPRIGHT: Unhappiness and dissatisfaction cast a shadow over your relationships. Dwelling too much upon the past will only make the situation worse. What you need is a renewal of vision and it will come if you are patient, but in the meantime, resist laying the blame for this situation on those around you. The problem lies within you.

REVERSED: Unexpected news arrives, and possibly in the form of a surprise visit from an old friend who will lift your spirits and suggest new ideas and ways forward. They may also remind you of past events that you would rather forget, but try if you can to learn their lessons.

Six of Cups

UPRIGHT: Nostalgia is likely to affect you as you become aware of just how many current events have their roots way back in your distant past. This is healthy up to a point because you will soon face a major life choice, and drawing upon the lessons of the past can help ensure that you make the right decision in the near future. Also, seek the advice of old friends.

REVERSED: The immediate future promises to be full of interesting options and possibilities, but you may miss out on them if you spend too much time dwelling on the past. Nostalgia can be taken too far.

Seven of Cups

UPRIGHT: Daydreaming threatens to distract you from pressing decisions that need to be made soon if you want to realize your hopes. Imagination is a wonderful faculty, but there is always a danger of it degenerating into mere wishful thinking. Divide your plans into distinct practical stages so that you can tell when they start to stray too far from reality.

REVERSED: The warnings attached to the upright seven are here more than doubled. Daydreaming is in danger of becoming delusion and if you do not seriously pay attention to reality, there are very real difficulties ahead.

Eight of Cups

UPRIGHT: Restlessness causes you to question many aspects of your life and possibly with good cause, as maybe it is time for some major changes. But remember that it is your own restlessness and need for a sense of purpose that is driving you. Others will not appreciate being blamed for what is basically your problem.

REVERSED: Gaiety, joy, and fellowship follow upon the realization of a dream achieved through perseverance and hard work. Difficult choices have been made and you have probably often wondered if you have been simply chasing a fantasy, but here you have the result.

Nine of Cups

UPRIGHT: Victory and success come your way as several long-held dreams come true. Share your good luck with others, and it will be multiplied. This is a good time for looking forward and making fresh plans for the future, because your confidence will be infectious. Several new and stimulating friends are likely to enter your life.

REVERSED: Your success is limited by miscalculation, imperfections, and carelessness. Complacency and an exaggerated sense of your importance spoil what should otherwise be a time of celebration, alienating many who would otherwise support you.

Ten of Cups

UPRIGHT: This card represents a happy home life, contentment at work, and good standing in your community, all of which are the result of diligent application and energy. You have established a stable and honored place for yourself and your loved ones in the world. Traditionally, this is the luckiest card in the Tarot for newlyweds.

REVERSED: Family disputes and bickering undermine your happiness and poison your relationships outside the family, too. The condition need not last, though, given enough patience and understanding.

Page of Cups

UPRIGHT: The Page of Cups is the ideal student – patient, receptive, docile, and eager to learn. Often the card represents the need for such an attitude if you are to progress. There are times for assertion and times for humility, and this is one of them. If it represents another person, it means someone nearby is willing to learn from you, although they may be too shy to ask.

REVERSED: The card represents an unwillingness to accept responsibility as fickleness, childishness, and self-absorption are masked as obedience. Such people can flatter others into taking them on, but will be unable to live up to the expectations they raise.

Knight of Cups

UPRIGHT: The Knight of Cups is romantic, loyal, generous, friendly, thoughtful, and idealistic. He inspires new ventures in both the romantic and practical fields without expecting much in return. This Knight is happiest when embarked upon some great spiritual quest like that of the Holy Grail. He signals the possibility of an idealistic new venture coming your way, possibly from an old friend.

REVERSED: Like all crushed romantics, the Knight reversed becomes cynical, bitter, deceitful, treacherous, and self-serving. The card symbolizes loss and the bitterness disappointment can bring, and its poisonous effect on relationships.

Queen of Cups

Upright: The Queen of Cups is warm, loving, sensitive, maternal, and eager to heal all the world's wounds. She is also practical, honest, and imaginative. Her imagination can be expressed through art, but more commonly through helping others relate to each other. Warm and playful, she is the ideal lover or parent because of her generosity and talent for putting people at ease.

Reversed: When reversed, the Queen shows her shadow side: arrogant, selfish, fickle, demanding, and unreasonable. As a lover she is both jealous and unfaithful, and she drains the energy and resources of everyone within her range.

King of Cups

Upright: The King is generous, honest, level-headed, kind, and cultured. He takes his responsibilities seriously and champions peace and the arts of civilization. He can be a formidable opponent in war, but only as a last resort. He is a great patron of the arts and sciences, and when in a favorable position in a spread his presence should be taken as encouragement to make plans on a grand scale.

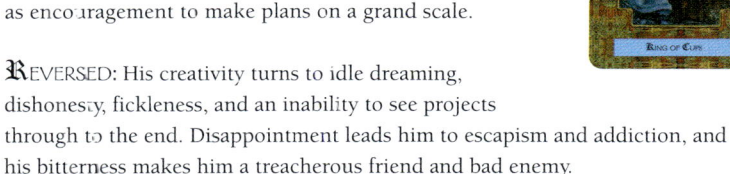

Reversed: His creativity turns to idle dreaming, dishonesty, fickleness, and an inability to see projects through to the end. Disappointment leads him to escapism and addiction, and his bitterness makes him a treacherous friend and bad enemy.

Ace of Wands

Upright: The Ace of Wands represents the beginning of some great new practical venture or career. The time is right for putting your boldest ideas into action, pushing back the boundaries of possibility, and sharing your enthusiasm with the world. Now, when everything is flowing your way, is the time to exercise your talents, stake out your territory, and show the world what you can do.

Reversed: The reversed Ace warns of the danger of getting too attached to new beginnings that haven't been thought through properly, of being unrealistic and not fully committed to your undertakings. There is a slim chance of success here, but only if you work at it.

Two of Wands

Upright: A possible partnership offers a way of furthering your ambitions. Unnecessary self-doubt is blocking your way, however, so you need to be decisive and trust in your instincts. Or, if this is not possible, ally yourself to someone who has that confidence. The prospects are good – just have faith.

Reversed: A possible disappointment from someone you have trusted leads you to question your own judgment. This does no harm as long as it is not taken too far. Make sure that any partners, in business and in personal relationships, are pulling their weight.

Three of Wands

Upright: Success and recognition are yours for the taking. Therefore, this is a good time for beginning new long-term enterprises, especially in the fields of arts and crafts, although it may be some time before the financial rewards come to you. Meanwhile, simply enjoy exercising your talents and have faith that others will equally enjoy what you do.

Reversed: A respite from current difficulties gives you time to marshal your forces. Beware the motives of those offering help, however, because they may simply be wanting to reap the benefits of all your efforts.

Four of Wands

Upright: It is now time for a well-deserved rest and the enjoyment of good company. Your plans were well-laid, so you can allow yourself to bask for a while as you see your ideas take shape in reality. This could also be a good time to consider moving house, or formalizing a romantic attachment. Enjoy this time, but don't allow complacency to creep in.

Reversed: Lack of co-operation from partners is likely to take the edge off life's pleasures just now, but be patient and persevering. It is not a serious problem, just one that requires tact, diplomacy, and a sense of your own worth.

Five of Wands

UPRIGHT: Gold, opulence, and splendor come your way, but a rival is threatening your position. Resist the urge to score points and your enemy will end up exposing their own pettiness. Competitiveness is healthy up to a point, but can become destructive if taken to extremes. Double-check everything you do, and the situation will resolve itself.

REVERSED: When the card is reversed, the situation becomes almost unbearable and it may be necessary to appeal to some higher authority to remove the threat, but be sure of your legal case before you do so.

Six of Wands

UPRIGHT: You benefit from triumphant and well-earned success as careful plans and hard work bear fruit. Be magnanimous in victory, and your moment of glory will be prolonged. This is no time for remembering petty insults and injuries suffered along the way because if you forget them, so will others.

REVERSED: Delays, treachery, and misunderstandings bring life to a standstill. Possible openings fail to materialize, and colleagues let you down. The only remedy for this disappointment is patience and good humor. The mood of the times will eventually change.

Seven of Wands

UPRIGHT: Success is likely, even though all the odds appear to be stacked against you. Victory will be all the sweeter for the effort it takes you, and sweeter still if you just quietly get on with doing whatever is necessary without complaint. Others may be trying to undermine you, but just talk things through with them openly and the threat will go away.

REVERSED: This is a time of doubt, hesitation, and uncertainty. You are on the right track, but lack the courage of your convictions and are likely to miss many of the opportunities that present themselves. Trust your instincts more.

Eight of Wands

UPRIGHT: The Eight indicates sudden progress that is possibly too fast for comfort, so try to slow things down a little and avoid over-hasty decisions that you might later regret. This is an exciting and well-starred time with travel, new business partnerships, and long-term romance all likely – just bear in mind that life is not always this easy, and plan for those rainy days.

REVERSED: Disharmony, quarrels, and rivalry all threaten to upset your plans. Rushed commitments come back to haunt you, and impatience could lead you into other choices that you will equally regret. Be cautious, and wait for the conditions to change.

Nine of Wands

Upright: You enjoy well-earned success gained through honesty, hard work, and intelligence. However, troubles are brewing on the horizon, and you are soon likely to be tested to the very limits of your patience and ability. Take the time now to cultivate key allies, and check too that your finances are robust enough to cope with unexpected demands.

Reversed: Here are the troubles warned of by the upright card. Be flexible and patient – you have the resources to cope and eventually turn the situation to your advantage. Beware of rash commitments, and safeguard your health.

Ten of Wands

Upright: Exhaustion threatens as you try to juggle the conflicting demands of work and family. Try to step back and reorganize your life in a more practical and realistic way, rather than just struggling on hopelessly against the tide of demands. Something has to give, and it need not necessarily be you.

Reversed: Difficulties and intrigues block your way when the card is reversed. You are likely to feel let down by someone you have trusted, although possibly this is your own fault for having abused their trust in the past. It is time to rethink the direction of your life.

Page of Wands

UPRIGHT: The Page of Wands is a messenger, usually of good fortune, heralding great events affecting your chosen career. He is energetic, loyal, idealistic, resourceful, and honest; the best kind of friend one could hope for. He can represent either the attitude you need in order to accomplish your aims – the part you must play toward someone of greater influence – or the person you should turn to for help to carry them out.

REVERSED: The reversed Page can represent either the imminence of bad news or the callowness and treachery of youth that fails to see projects through to the end, or twists information into mischief-making gossip.

Knight of Wands

UPRIGHT: The Knight of Wands is a versatile warrior, armed and fearlessly ready for action. The card signifies departures, change, and adventures into the unknown. It's a warning to keep your eyes and ears open, because you are surrounded by challenge. But if, like the Knight (or with his help), you face it with courage, flexibility, and imagination, there's every reason that you should triumph in the end.

REVERSED: Disruption, conflict, quarrels, and sudden upheavals, either geographical or emotional, are indicated. Expect the painful breaking of old ties, either because of your own fickleness or someone else's.

Queen of Wands

UPRIGHT: The Queen of Wands is a mature, practical person with a great down-to-earth wisdom. Charming, sympathetic, and graceful, she is less outgoing than her bold King but has very strong character and self-possession. She gets things done by talking to individuals rather than groups, and thus getting below the surface of events. Often she is the real leader of a group without it being noticed.

REVERSED: This Queen becomes petty, cruel, and domineering. Her emotions become fickle, leading to possible infidelity. Instead of listening to others, she tries to force her own wishes on them through bullying and manipulation; a dangerous enemy.

King of Wands

UPRIGHT: The King of Wands is a charming leader who is energetic, honest, diplomatic, and generous. His fatherliness can tend toward being too trusting. Being naturally loyal and conscientious, he is a great friend in times of trouble, being unafraid to take up arms in a good cause. In a spread he can represent either the attitude needed to address the situation, or the person you should turn to for help.

REVERSED: The King reversed becomes severe, demanding, temperamental, intolerant, and aggressive, prone to being prejudiced and overbearing. This card can signal the danger of a dispute with someone both powerful and unwilling to see your point of view.

Ace of Pentacles

The Ace of Pentacles represents perfect contentment and is often considered the luckiest card in the pack. The benefits are mainly material, but should promote a general sense of well-being that spills over into the emotional and spiritual spheres. This is a good time for beginning a new business venture or career. It can mean an unexpected windfall that will enable you to realize long-cherished dreams.

Reversed: Modest gain or empty prosperity, the curse of Midas, is forecast. If you neglect to share out any good fortune that comes your way it could end in loneliness. Alternatively, the card may warn of being at the mercy of a greedy and selfish person.

Two of Pentacles

Upright: Difficulty and embarrassment at the beginning of a new business venture is suggested by this card, but the prospects are very promising if you are prepared to put in the hard work and resist making reckless gambles. Times of change like this are full of opportunity but also risk, so be prepared for a rollercoaster of a journey!

Reversed: Although there is a sense of unreality surrounding some current relationships, it is worth persevering – however, do watch out for ulterior motives in your partners. Get all agreements down in writing so that there can be no arguments later.

Three of Pentacles

Upright: A very promising outlook for new ventures is forecast, which calls for the exercise of all your best talents. Creativity flourishes in this situation, so bring out the artist or craftsman in you and do your best. You have a chance to prove your mastery to the world and reap the rewards. Integrity is everything.

Reversed: A proposal is in danger of coming to nothing. Sloppiness and haste threaten to spoil what could have been a creative and rewarding venture. You need to concentrate and stop imagining that the world automatically owes you anything.

Four of Pentacles

Upright: Due reward comes after a long struggle, but you need to shrug off any lingering bitterness or sense of grievance if you are to enjoy it. There is some danger of you becoming a miser. Enjoy your good fortune, but also share it with others who probably did far more for you during the difficult times than you realized.

Reversed: Obstacles on the material front are exacerbated, and possibly even created, by your eagerness for money. There is more to life than this – begin by taking pride in your work purely for its own sake, and you may just find that this helps toward attaining a decent reward for it.

Five of Pentacles

Upright: Traditionally this is a financially unlucky card, indicating problems and possible unemployment. Often these are caused simply by the fear of them happening, so you might be creating your own bad luck. By way of compensation, your love life should blossom, so try to be less materialistic. Occasionally, though, the card can signal a windfall.

Reversed: Financial strain, or a slight gain, comes with unwelcome strings attached. There is a real danger of money worries causing a major relationship to degenerate, but the real problem is your own attitude, not the lack of money itself.

Six of Pentacles

Upright: Financial success comes your way and justice demands that you pass the favor along. Just as others have taken a gamble on your talents, now it's time for you to do the same, either by sponsoring some struggling aspirant or simply by sharing some of your profits with the less fortunate in the world.

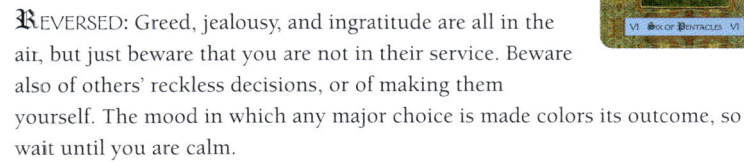

Reversed: Greed, jealousy, and ingratitude are all in the air, but just beware that you are not in their service. Beware also of others' reckless decisions, or of making them yourself. The mood in which any major choice is made colors its outcome, so wait until you are calm.

Seven of Pentacles

Upright: The Seven foretells a truly rewarding time. The possibilities before you are quite awesome, but do think in the long-term. Decide who you are and what you would like to be remembered for by your family and friends. The choices you face really are that important. Destiny is at work.

Reversed: Strife and disorder threaten through lack of a sense of direction and clear purpose. In the end no one else can say exactly what you have to do right now; because some decisions have to be made alone. Bear in mind, however, that self-pity is always the worst advisor.

Eight of Pentacles

Upright: Success and the calm mastery of your talents are at hand. You are appreciated by those you work with and are likely to receive your just rewards. Be prudent, though, as this is a time for consolidation and not wild excess. You are offered the chance of rewarding adventure, but you are also expected to be responsible in your actions.

Reversed: There is a danger of wasting the opportunities in front of you through vanity and indiscipline. Thinking purely in the short term means that you are likely to miss a very real chance to make a worthwhile impact upon the world. Avoid borrowing money just now.

Nine of Pentacles

UPRIGHT: You are likely to receive substantial reward for your accomplishments, and you will be able to afford to relax and enjoy your more contemplative inclinations. Don't shut out your family and friends, however, because they have had to put up with your darker moods and have probably helped you through them much more than you know.

REVERSED: This signals a time of struggle, with barely adequate rewards and all kinds of unforeseen dangers and deceptions threatening to disrupt your life. Past immoralities may now catch up with you and demand their price.

Ten of Pentacles

UPRIGHT: This card signifies success, completion, and an invitation to rest on your laurels – although not for too long. You have worked hard to gain your present position and you are entitled to enjoy the benefits, and not least the space, to enjoy family life. However, nothing lasts forever, so you should also start making fresh plans for the future.

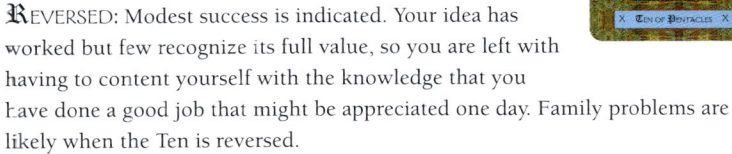

REVERSED: Modest success is indicated. Your idea has worked but few recognize its full value, so you are left with having to content yourself with the knowledge that you have done a good job that might be appreciated one day. Family problems are likely when the Ten is reversed.

Page of Pentacles

Upright: Intuitive, sensitive, creative, and hard-working, the Page is a successful student with psychic tendencies of which he is not always conscious. The card can signify good news such as success in a test or examination, or the attitude needed to make it happen. He can be a bit of a dreamer, though, so engrossed in whatever project he is focussed upon that everyday life may fall apart around him.

Reversed: The dreaminess of the upright Page becomes a curse and the Page tries to compensate by becoming prickly and demanding over things that do not really matter, lacking any true sense of proportion. He becomes unreliable and selfish.

Knight of Pentacles

Upright: The Knight of Pentacles is useful, reliable, patient, persistent, and loyal. He is cautious by nature, preferring evolution to revolution, but has courage enough when it is called for. He is not a great one for spiritual quests, preferring prizes you can hold in the hand over those of the heart and soul. A happy measure of wealth may come your way, but beware reckless spending.

Reversed: The card represents stagnation, cowardice, inertia, and laziness. It shows a life in danger of losing its way through idleness and lack of imagination, cultivating narrow prejudices about others that sooner or later backfire.

Queen of Pentacles

Upright: The Queen of Pentacles is regal, generous, and diplomatic, ruling her suit in close partnership with her King and in much the same manner, although with perhaps a touch more warmth and understanding of human frailty. She has a good grasp of finances as well as being a generous and welcoming hostess. The card represents either someone you should turn to, or qualities you need to cultivate.

Reversed: The Queen becomes greedy, spiteful, extravagant, suspicious, demanding, and full of complaints about the ingratitude of the world. She is blind to others' good intentions. Beware of succumbing to her oddly persuasive views.

King of Pentacles

Upright: The King of Pentacles is wealthy, confident, commanding, inspiring, intelligent, mathematical, straightforward, and determined. He is conservative, hard-working, and leads by example. He is equivalent to Jupiter in astrology, the jovial ruler of the other planets and bounteous dispenser of wealth, which he naturally attracts. He is a loyal friend, a wise counsellor, and a reliable, if cautious, partner.

Reversed: This King is insensitive, greedy, calculating, devious, jealous, and aggressive – a dangerous enemy when in a position of authority, because he will use any means at all to get his own way.

Acknowledgments

Special thanks go to Roger and Linda Garland for the wonderful card designs that bring this Tarot to life. As ever, they were a complete pleasure and inspiration to work with. Also to Liz Dean for her tactful editing, and everyone else at CICO Books who made this project possible. For more on the background to this particular pack and Tarot in general, visit the companion website at www.unicorngarden.com/tarot.

Nigel Suckling